PROPELLED

TO

GREATNESS

HOPE THROUGH

TURBULENT

STORMS

MARISSA DANDRIDGE

PROPELLED TO GREATNESS
Hope Through Turbulent Storms

Marissa Dandridge
Post Office Box 221
Rochester, Illinois 62563-9998
scribing7@gmail.com

Copyright ©2021
ISBN: 978-1-949027-55-6

Published by Destined To Publish
www.DestinedToPublish.com

DEDICATION

For every individual who has
encountered turbulent storms (of life).

Turbulence: marked by bursts
of destructive force or intense activity

ACKNOWLEDGMENTS

First, I would like to acknowledge God for never giving up on me and for His tender mercies and grace.

My expression of gratitude goes out to my husband, son, and daughter for their support and encouragement. You are awesome, and I sincerely appreciate and love you.

A special thanks to Marilyn Alexander with Destined to Publish and her awesome team, who assisted me with yet another opportunity to publish my work.

I want to thank my headship Apostle George G. Smith and Prophetess Dawn Smith of Kingdom Authority Ministries International for their loving kindness and encouragement.

To all the individuals who assisted me during this walk, thank you.

Thanks to everyone else who has encouraged me along the way.

CONTENTS

INTRODUCTION

My husband and I had just purchased our first house. We had worked diligently to get out of debt. For nearly 14 years, we both had experienced the effects of addiction, him longer than me. Our past hurts and life experiences were part of the equation, but we were desperate to get beyond it. We wanted more than what we'd had before, and we wanted to be in a place other than where we had been in the past. It was time for us to move up. And we were filled with excitement. I felt like we were the people on the show called *The Jeffersons*, with the theme song that goes, "Well, we're moving on up, to the East Side … we finally got a piece of the pie."

Not too long after we had purchased the house and moved in, trouble hit. It was as though storm after storm after storm hit us one by one. I just wanted to scream, "I can't believe this! Are you freaking kidding me? What in the world is going on around me?" The time of celebrating was interfered with by what I thought was my husband's past addictions and other troubles that were magnified. As I sought out better employment opportunities, I was met with opposition. Nothing seemed to be going right, and my trials and tribulations were great. I was in a car accident that totaled my van. The pain was taxing, both emotionally and physically. Seeking God and expecting Him to heal me required me to come to a place of totally trusting and depending upon Him. I found myself in a dark place as I tried to take matters into my own hands. These situations caused me to become unloving at times. Yet there was hope through these storms.

In the book The Love Dare by Stephen and Alex Kendrick, I read: "Love is hard to offend and quick to forgive... To be *irritable* means 'to be near the point of a knife'... People who are irritable are locked, loaded, and ready to overreact." I had found myself being irritable and not quick to show love.

One day, I found myself pouring my heart out to God and inviting Him to visit with me. I cried because of my guilt and shame and anger. At times, I had become hopeless. I could not see how the future would come about with my mixed feelings regarding my marriage, job, and relationships with people and with God. Where was I supposed to go from here?

Let me lead you to a place of victory through storms. My hope and trust had to be placed in God. He was my hope when I was hopeless: *"I will lift up mine eyes unto the hills, from whence cometh my help"* (Psalm 121:1 KJV). God is never too far away.

CHAPTER I
HOUSE PURCHASE

My husband and I both lived in small towns when we were younger. He grew up in southern Illinois, and I grew up in Kentucky. Both communities consisted of close family and friends. We were both considered the "black sheep" in our families, but I discovered that the troubles we faced at a young age would push us towards our destiny. Many events or experiences in my young life were not so good or could not be recalled. For instance, I do not recall celebrating any Thanksgiving holidays. The only things I remember about Christmas were waking up at Granny Tammy's house on Christmas Day alongside my sisters and getting a homemade dark brown Cabbage Patch-like doll with black hair. That was the extent of my memories of those holidays. I remember my uncles who lived there, but they disappeared one day. I did not recall any goodbyes or hugs; they were just gone. Although I stayed with Granny sometimes and at Ma Lucy's house other times, most of my memories were either awful or nonexistent.

There used to be a pile of rubbish or straw-like grass in the right corner of the backyard. Several times, I made my way back there only to find some round, brown balls. So, I gathered them and sat on a step on the tiny back porch. As I squeezed a few of them, gooey stuff came out. I decided to do the same with the rest of them. As I stared at them, I became curious as to what they were. Later, I discovered that they were hen eggs. I never knew eggs could be brown. Sometimes, while in the back yard, to keep from being bored, I would walk on those large, brown, empty thread spools – well, cable reels. It was exciting for me.

There were several small families in the area where I lived with Ma. One day, a boy, who had to be at least seven years older than me, saw me sitting by a tree in front of the house, but not too close to the house. He came over and knelt next to me and made small talk with me. Then he asked me if I wanted to see his penis. Well, what in the world was that, anyway? He then pulled it out of his pants, but something or someone broke up that situation. After that moment, there were other encounters that would later spark my interest in sex. One young lady at a sleepover exposed her pubic hair and asked me if I wanted to feel her "bush." She then took my hand and placed it inside of her underwear. My sisters and I lay in the bed with her; I just remember lying on her right side. The family we were left with must have been familiar and trusted by either Ma, Granny, or both, but I had no idea who these people were.

One good memory at Ma's house was when my uncle Rowland came to visit. He and his wife, my aunt, would come and visit, and they always brought us McDonald's. Such treats were few and far between. My heart overflowed with joy to see them but saddened quickly upon their departure.

I stayed at Granny's and at Ma's. I did not really understand why I had two homes. Granny was a nurse, and she knew how to care for us. She took care of other adults and children in their homes. She had lost a son, Uncle Wilson, who was my favorite uncle, although he spanked me quite often for acting unwisely. When I was at Granny's, I recall seeing a black shadow walk in front of me. I believed that was my uncle Wilson's ghost that was there. There was a black statue that I had, which I played with often. It was close to nine inches tall, skinny and shiny, and I treasured it. I called it a booty ball. My uncle's nickname was Booty – perhaps I had named it after him.

As time went on, my family moved to Chicago and then to the Quad Cities. From there, I went to college. Upon entrance to college, I was soon distracted: I fell in love (or lust) with a beautiful man. He was a fine and sexy-looking man to me. I wanted to get to know him from the first time we set eyes on one another in a tutoring session. I soon began to date him; I remember speaking the words, "I want you to be my husband." I wanted him bad, and I had my idea of a perfect family. I wanted one husband who would give me children; I did not want several children by different men. I wanted a beautiful house. I pictured us being like the families on *The Brady Bunch and Little House on the Prairie.*

When I declared that he would be my husband, I did not know that according to Job 22:28-29, if I decreed a thing, it would be or come to pass. In other words, what I had spoken over my life was going to come to pass. I literally spoke this into existence.

My husband's mother was a nurse. He had much love for her. As I cherished my granny, he had also cherished his grandmother. They were both filled with wisdom. His father was well known, and he admired him as well. Although they spent time together as fishermen, it was not without the presence of alcohol. Their time together at the bars was the perfect opportunity for learned behavior: drinking alcohol. Along with this came the witnessing of his father's fury and abusive behavior towards others, something else he learned from his father.

My husband had experiences with spirits as well. When he was a young boy, his grandmother warned him not to enter a nearby house, but curiosity got the best of him. He soon began to see in a whole new realm. As he lived, there were several misfortunes or tragedies, untold pains that left a scar on his soul and would affect several years of his life. As he grew and attempted to move on and forget, he joined the military. Once a Marine, always a Marine, but with much anger and alcohol. Both the alcohol and the anger intensified upon the death and burial of his beloved father. As the years passed, he was determined to be college bound, but some of his troubles followed.

Although we had both wanted a better life, we bought our life experiences along. After his mother, grandmother, and some other relatives passed before and after college, the familiar spirits came to comfort or make themselves known to him, just

4

as my uncle Wilson's so-called spirit did with me. Although I knew they really were not sent of God, my husband seemed to want to hold dear those familiar presences. Determined to move on, little did we know we were living our past together, bringing it into our future.

Ambition

As time passed, we came up with a brilliant idea: we wanted to purchase a house. After enduring many storms, we were finally able to make that purchase. What an accomplishment this was for us. We had lived off government funds in the past. We did not graduate from college on schedule. We had childcare bills and low-paying jobs, and the cars we drove were not the best. Our run-ins with Section 8 landlords and issues were overwhelming. We just got tired of dealing with the same old things. We wanted more for our children and for ourselves – we wanted more than what our parents had for us. So yes, our first house purchase was a major milestone for us. We could only move up from here.

My husband and I may not have been the first in our families to own a house, we may have married after having children, we may have had many debts and other hardships, but it took determination on our behalf to get to this point. My husband and I had been working tirelessly on our marriage, keeping our family together, and buying our first house. The kids would have their own rooms. I was looking forward to the new journey, but I could not help but think about the words a lady said to me some months before the purchase. She was a counselor at a facility in a nearby town. She stared into my eyes and said, "He is not ready yet." She told me that he needed more help. I wanted to believe her, but I disregarded those words. My hopes were high. This lady, no matter what degree she had earned or what training she had, was not going to run my marriage. It was clear to me that she just did not want to see us succeed. I had hope and faith in my husband. Everything was going to be simply fine. I believed Psalm 33:20 (NLT): *"We put our hope in the Lord. He is our help and our shield."*

Shortly after we had purchased our house, we put much effort into getting it up to par. I had so many creative ideas for decorating. But day after day, my focus began to shift, because I noticed that every day, my husband would go to work and then come home to work on the house. He had become fixated. He worked tirelessly to get the house all fixed up, barely making time to eat, sleep, or attend church. I was so angry. I experienced fatigue and was short tempered. The excitement of the purchase and being a first-time homeowner was now becoming more burdensome to me. Making our house a home was stressing me out. His time was so consumed by it that there was little time for his family. Our first family home, yet we were barely living together as a family. Surely, this would pass… again.

My thoughts became more focused on how stressful this must be for him. I began to think about my role as a wife to see that he was the man of the house who was trying to get everything together. I was trying to be sensitive. I was trying to give him the benefit of the doubt. My feelings had to be pushed to the side, but my heart was relieved when my husband called on a friend to assist in upgrading the house. We had to get rid of those rooster cabinets and make the restroom downstairs more functional. The house was perfect for me and my family; I just wanted to enjoy the journey to make it our own. My view was not the same as my husband's, "Mr. Fix-It." There was yardwork that needed to be taken care of and some other minor repairs in and around the house. Fat hope was canceled as I watched my husband constantly finding something wrong and becoming more anxious. The more anxious he became, the more upset I became. The more upset I became, the more I became irritated as a mother and wife. The joy of dwelling there had become more burdensome to me. All I could wonder was, could that lady have been right? Now, I was beginning to be regretful. I hated being wrong, but I sure could not believe that the life we used to live, the lifestyle of the addict, was suddenly catching up with us. My stomach was churning. I was crying deep within.

My heart was crumbling within me as I began to reminisce of the days of old. My husband and I had separated several times over the course of our marriage. Oh, how addiction is real! The last time we separated, I had cried many nights. Although my love for him was great, there were times I wished I would die in the fight. My heart longed for my lover, but the heartache of living with him was costly. Most nights and days, my mind wandered. Who is he with? Will he be found dead? Will he call me from jail? Does he want a divorce? Will he become violent with me again? It was difficult for me to concentrate on myself and the children. If I sat still for too long or if I was not busy enough, my mind would become consumed with stories that were not real. Fantasizing was extremely easy for me, and it was uncontrollable. I would create mental images of myself catching my husband loving on another woman. Then, my reaction was to become very confrontational and fight the woman and threaten to beat her up. Most of the time, I would create situations in my head like "If he does… then I am going to do…" or "If he says… then I am going to say…"

I was draining myself physically, and mostly because my focus was misguided. Sometimes, I would fantasize about how my husband and I would walk together holding hands and having the most wonderful time with our children. When my husband was sober, even for a few seconds, I was happy. When he was drunk, I was angry, even if I did not express my feelings. My emotions were on a roller coaster – "a situation or experience that alternates between making you feel excited, exhilarated, or happy and making you feel sad, disappointed, or desperate" (www.collinsdictionary.com).

One day, I had worked myself up so much that my emotions were really running rampant. Our children were with their godmother that evening. It was at that time that I decided to make an unannounced visit to my husband's place. My heart was racing, and a 15-minute drive felt like an eternity. It was getting dark out. My nervous system was overactive. My prayers were that no police were out and that they would not be called due to any unforeseen circumstances. Upon my arrival, I hurried and got out of the car. I knocked hard on the door several times before he asked who it was. I responded by saying, "Marissa." I could hear a little conversation going on inside. When he opened the door, he had an alarming look on his face. I began to lecture him. It appeared to me that my words were never-ending. He had company that was sitting with him in the living room quietly. I began to confront my husband about the alcohol they both were drinking. My mouth and emotions were working overtime.

My attention then turned to the woman who was sitting on the chair. I looked at her and approached her as I asked my husband why he had this woman up in this house. The individual said with a somewhat angry and offended voice, "Excuse me, miss, but I ain't no woman, I'm a man." My eyes could not have been mistaken. Instantaneously, there was a sound of tranquility in the room. No movement and no voices. My husband then said, after I asked who this guy was, that he (my husband) was lonely and wanted company because he just did not want to be alone. He had invited the individual to have drinks and sit and talk with him. He just met this guy at a gas station. Suddenly, the tranquility left the room as I fussed about that. My husband told the guy that he had to go. He drove him to a nearby gas station and came back immediately. I told him that I just could not keep doing this and he had to change. But then I pushed my emotions to the side and began to feel sorry for him. All I could think about was how lonely he was and how I was still his wife. I felt sorry for him. How could I live without him? He could not stop drinking. He needed me! Huh!

We went our separate ways the next morning. All I could think about was how I was gonna continue. As I began to put the kids' bunk beds up, he pulled into the driveway... just wasted. A weight would have been lifted from me if the person I depended on – my husband – had been sober enough to just help me finish getting the beds together. As an argument broke out, I cried. I hated to see him arrive in this condition, but I was glad to see him go. Lord! When I walked into the living room, a guy named Henry pulled into the driveway. To make everything appear to be OK, I put on a happy face, but he saw right through my fake smile and expressions. He looked directly into my eyes and told me that my husband was too preoccupied and would not leave me in a place of frustration (from what I can remember him saying). He spoke calmly and told me he saw (prophetically) what was going on. When he left, a load was lifted.

I was striving to work hard and stay focused. My husband, my children, and my marriage remained dear to me. I did not want to be part of the statistics: black and divorced, children by multiple partners, and poor. But I was fighting against demonic powers. My husband and I had conflicting spirits. We fought physically, cursed and blessed, and had vain imaginations, but

I would still be pressing to do right by God. Philippians 3:14 (KJV) says, *"I press toward the mark for the prize of the high calling of God in Christ Jesus."* My husband had to see me truly following Christ so he could see and desire Christ.

I remember our good friend Henry told me that my husband would be attacked three times as badly as before if he went back to his old ways. We showed up at Henry's house one day because he was very spiritual and prophetic. I was concerned because my husband had expressed in great desperation and agony regarding how demons were in his head messing with him. When we left that house, although there was such hope and encouragement for the two of us, I did not know how much I would have to engage our unseen enemy. Continuing to work on our house, many times, I was wondering if everything was about to blow up in my face. I could see that we were heading back to a very familiar place. I could just taste it, even though we were giving our beautiful home a makeover. We both began to take offense to comments and jokes that we were making towards one another and about various situations. It appeared that almost everything that was being said was fighting words. I could not keep my mouth shut, and I could barely keep myself from wanting to strike (to engage in battle with him). Who was I becoming?

Although we had just purchased a new house, I was also searching for different employment. The school district called me one day, and I applied and was hired as a substitute assistant to the classroom teacher. After a few years, and after getting my bachelor's degree, I moved on. Although I was still working with the school district, I was going to work while hearing "Miss Marissa" all day long, Monday through Friday. When I got off work and went home, I was hearing "Mommy" and "Marissa" the rest of the evening. Not only that, but things were also falling apart at the daycare and I needed to make more money. My husband tried to convince me to apply for a job with the government. But I had heard his complaints about how he had been treated as a government worker, and I saw how he was laid off during some weeks over the summer, and I just did not want to go through that. There was so much news regarding the government – I just could not put my faith in the government at that time. Besides that, I did not want to keep job hopping. My goal was to have good insurance, become established in a good job, save money, and be satisfied with the job.

The Rehab Center

My life was becoming even more grueling. One day, a coworker told me about a job that she had applied for. She told me that she was going to be hired at a rehab center and that she would get a bonus if I was hired there too. I was not so sure that I wanted to work there, but I ended up applying and getting hired. I worked the night shift and was assigned mainly with the youth. My training was done in a short amount of time. What was I doing working at a rehab center? I had been through so much abuse in the past. It seemed nearly impossible to confront others who had the same disrespect that I had encountered at home. My flesh would have to be under control, and I would not be able to raise my voice, cry, throw things, or lash out in any way when faced with similar situations at work. How could I keep others from knowing about my personal experience with the addiction world? How could I deal with others and their addictions? What challenges would I face?

I worked 12:00 to 8:00 AM for the first time at the center. I thought I would have a difficult time staying awake, especially after not having uninterrupted sleep from 5:00 PM to 11:30 PM. I took a half-hour break at 4:05 AM to get a cappuccino. I felt well rested, but I did not know how my body would react to working the third shift.

Working new hours along with everything that had been going on, I felt as though I should have been more relaxed and in line with the Word of God, but I was not. I was having trouble keeping my mind on positive things. As strange as this sounds, I had been thinking about what I was thinking about, and it was all negative. I could not help but wonder if my children were safe, or if men and women were hanging out at my house partying. Would a fight break out? Would the police or paramedics be called? My mind was just racing. I looked up scriptures on the mind. Isaiah 26:3 (NKJV): *"You will keep him in perfect peace, whose mind is stayed on You, because he trusts in You."* Philippians 4:7 (NKJV): *"And the peace of God, which surpasses all understanding, will guard your hearts and minds through Christ Jesus.* " These were immensely helpful in guiding me.

I had been working at the center making at least $4,000 a year more than the job at the daycare. I recently received a job offer from juvenile probation. They would pay me nearly $10,000 more than what I was currently making. I turned down the offer and continued to work the night shift, under the impression that when my six-month probationary period was up, I would get a raise. That was not what occurred. I needed better insurance coverage as well. So, my stay was for a short while longer.

This job was a challenge mainly due to the hours and my home life. One day while making my nightly rounds, I was walking through a unit that I was assigned to, and I saw an orange industrial extension cord across the floor in a room. That was against the facility rules, so I took the cord from the room. The next morning, just before the end of my shift, I heard someone screaming and cursing and yelling my name. I then heard the staff running towards the youth. After he was calmed down, I later found out that his roommate had gotten him all worked up that morning by telling him that I had lifted his blanket and viewed him in his underwear.

As I continued to work nights, I heard the Lord speaking to me about writing my first book. He spoke continually regarding what I needed to write. On my days off and throughout the day at home, the journey of writing my first book, *Uprooted*, began. I had to focus on what God wanted me to share with the world.

Every time I began to write and think about writing, it appeared the gates of hell were prevailing against me. There were several occasions when I thought this was too much. I recall wondering why the phone or doorbell would ring, I felt tired, someone would knock on the door, or some other form of distraction would take place. My train of thought was off as the distractions would come. How could God allow all these distractions if He wanted me to write a book?

I soon discovered after working the night shift that chaos had been breaking out in my home like never before. Who was at my house drinking? What was the evidence of other women and/or men being in my home? My anger became kindled. I found strands of hair that were not mine. Cigarette smoke had invaded my home. I felt an uprising (riot) coming forth from within me. My heart was angered to the core. I knew how I left my house, so I knew when things were out of order. There was some shady stuff going on. My blood pressure was elevated. This was betrayal. I was not allowed to leave work to go home for lunch because the 24-hour facility rule meant that a certain number of individuals had to be on staff always. So, I could not play the full role of a detective like I really wanted to, but rest assured, something was up.

Whenever I was at home, I enjoyed rearranging my furniture and cleaning house. I would rearrange at least every thirty days, and I would make sure that the furniture had equal space on each side and that the area rug was lined up with the lines on the hardwood floor. The food seasoning had to be arranged by color. I had a hair, body, and general supply shelf in the hall closet. If any item was out of order, I would know it and would have to correct it each time. I had become a perfectionist – a busybody.

The sound of glass bottles clinging in the kitchen garbage can was a familiar sound. It was the instrumental sound of those alcohol bottles buried at the bottom of the can that were rubbing against one another. Every time I heard the sound, that meant that there were more bottles of alcohol around. No matter how many times I searched the house and threw the bottles out, it seemed as though they just kept multiplying. My life was always consumed by getting rid of every single evidence of alcoholism. I just hated the sound. Hearing it almost sent me into a trance. It appears my mind began to go back to the old experiences.

We were all behaving differently. I was trying to look at the spiritual and natural side of things as I tried to figure out what was going on. Miscellaneous phone numbers showing up all over the house? Huh! What exactly was going on when I was away from home? Oh my God! I could only imagine the worst. There was no way that I could go through the drama that came with this drinking again. Things were "hidden in plain sight."

Things were getting shakier. My God! That lady was right when she had warned me that "he was not ready." Deep down inside, I knew it, but I was hoping she was so wrong. It had become increasingly difficult to communicate with my husband. For every concern that I had and brought to his attention, he had an excuse. So, why did I slowly began to see things his way? It was as though I had begun to see things through his lenses. I did not trust what God was saying and showing me. God's voice was altered by my doubts. Maybe I was overreacting because I was tired or because I refused to trust Him. Maybe everything that I was seeing was wrong.

Well, dang! Talk about short lived. How many times could I say that? My conversations and ideas were so focused on my husband. I was trying so hard to make him change. I was driving myself crazy because he did not respond to me the way I wanted him to. I was a bit frustrated with my husband one day when I asked him to help me clean the house. He asked me, "Why?" I told him, "Because it's a mess." He then responded by saying there is a lot of work he does around the house that I don't see. He told me that he cleaned and scrubbed the oil off the back of the wall behind the stove. My response was to let him know that I needed help keeping the house together. Laundry was something that had to be kept up with, as well as dusting and sweeping, mopping the floors, and cleaning both bathrooms and the living room. He told me that he did not understand why we were going through this again and that a lot of times, I would just start a job around the house and not finish it. He told me that I would just let the mail pile up instead of throwing it away after opening and reading it. It was then that I told him to forget it.

All I wanted was for him to help me clean the house, and the conversation turned into a huge ordeal. My goodness! It seemed as though all of my hard work was going unnoticed. Why couldn't he even appreciate me posting scriptures around the house? Posting the scriptures around the house helped me daily, and I could not wrap my mind around why he thought it was hard to clean the sticky residue off the walls and mirrors. After he stated that he cooked most of the time, I asked him why we had to go through all this conversation just because I asked him for one thing: to help me around the house. Stupid situations like these annoyed me. My character was being tried. I wanted to explode. I decided to assign chores for the children to do. They were to wash their laundry and the bathroom sinks, wash dishes, and sweep and mop the kitchen floor. I had to do something to keep myself from getting so frustrated.

I was working thirty-seven and a half hours each week. What high expectations my husband wanted, for me to keep the entire house clean. I did not understand why it was such an issue for me not to assist with taking out the garbage on Thursdays, cutting the grass, and fixing things around the house when it is broken. What if I only tended to the house occasionally? The house would continue to be a disaster.

There was so much craziness around my husband and me. Many situations arose. I remember expressing to my husband, especially earlier on in our marriage, how I would dream or think that someone would die, and they would end up dying. One day, we learned that my husband's uncle Lenny died. The refrigerator had broken down. People on the job seemed to be complaining about me more and more. Almost everyone around me was irritating me. I bounced two checks. Two doctors prescribed eight medications for our son. My PMS was off. My husband and I were not being very affectionate. Someone backed up and hit my van while it was parked. My husband did not get the full-time permanent position that he was hoping for. Could things have been any crazier? What was this hell around me? There appeared to be an unquenchable fire around me, and not the unquenchable fire of the Holy Spirit. I was enduring unsettled circumstances. I felt like a pregnant woman who was in labor. Oh, the pain.

Through all of this, I found myself struggling with loving others. I found myself not wanting to be bothered with people, not even holding conversations. I just found it difficult to engage in a conversation for longer than five minutes at a time. Quite often, I felt the need to curse, but deep down inside, I knew that was not something I should really do. I wanted to serve and honor God with all that I had because He was all that I needed. I wanted to be stronger and wiser in Christ Jesus.

One weekend, I went to church. After praise and worship and speaking to others, I felt powerful. I felt even more powerful after listening to part of Joel Osteen's message on taking on the strength of God for battle. I was amazed. I truly felt that God was telling me that all I had to do was speak to Him and fight using His strength and not my own. I decided to order the DVD.

I needed to know God intimately. I wanted to start researching scriptures that dealt with songs that I enjoyed singing. I hated being in a dry place. One thing was for sure, God wanted me to continue journaling so that more of my life story would be shared. I had my book written out, and I had several title possibilities, knowing that the title of the book would need to draw people to take a closer look at what was inside. Not only was I to write and be published, but I would speak in front of groups about my life story. It was then that I imagined myself doing the work of an evangelist and seeing people healed. In this vision of myself, I would be well dressed in unique, yet nicely designed clothing. My hair and eyeglasses would make me look very professional, and the glory of God would just surround me. People would feel the presence of God's anointing just by being next to me and hearing me speak and sing.

It was time to go to work again. While I slept before going in, I had the strangest, weirdest dream. It was a bit nerve-racking. I dreamed that me, my children, acquaintances, family members, and strangers were outside for some type of gathering when suddenly, the sky became dark and grayish, kind of like a tornado. The clouds were rolling in quickly. I heard awful screaming from the sky, screaming that was bothersome. It was like the scream of someone's tortured soul. Suddenly, I looked up with tears in my eyes while covering up a young girl, possibly my daughter, and I saw a lady with a red dress on that was mixed up in the clouds, and I was behind her trying to snatch her purse. Suddenly, there was a loud thunder. The cloud departed, the lady and the man was sucked up, and then the clouds came back together. I woke up after the alarm went off. I was confused by what I saw in my sleep, and it was a bit disturbing. I immediately wanted to know what that dream meant. I just did not understand. Was God trying to tell me something?

As I was coming home from work the next morning, I was asking God to show me myself. I wanted Him to show me any darkness that was inside of my heart. After doing dorm checks at midnight at work, I began to read where I had left off in Joyce Meyer's book A Leader in The Making. As I began to read the ninth paragraph, God showed me that I was struggling with the very thing that I had just prayed about. Part of this paragraph said, "We must let the Holy Spirit examine our hearts and show us any wrong attitude that is in us – and let Him root that thing out and change us." I was just shocked. In chapter 5 of the book, there is a section called "Negative Conditions of The Heart." I could not stop reading the chapter once I had begun.

As God dealt with me in this area, it was my belief that He was going to do something great, and that my husband and I were about to see the results. I was still trusting God for the promises that He made. With multiple callings God placed upon my life as a pastor's wife (to be), worship leader, intercessory prayer, teacher, worshipper, and whatever else God wanted to reveal to me, I just knew that God required more of me. But these roles seemed almost impossible to fulfill. At least, they seemed so farfetched. I was just so excited about that. One thing I did believe was that I was going to stay in God's presence and word and not allow so much fussing in my household. Praying that I and my household would line up with the Word of God was vital.

With a newly found confidence, I began to purchase and wear real gold, wear makeup, and get my hair, nails, and eyebrows done regularly. This was challenging for me. I had always been a tomboy, and shopping was never my thing. Sweats and jeans were my thing. All these new things were totally outside of my comfort zone. As I began to make all those improvements, one thing was for sure, my husband hardly even noticed the changes. So, this was short-lived for me. I felt as though it was my duty to become more attractive to him. I was trying to do this not only as a wifely duty, but to make my husband love me more. It was as though I was singing the lyrics from the song "I'm Gonna Make You Love Me" repeatedly. My confidence and beauty had slowly become rooted in how I perceived his reaction towards me. Even though I wanted to honor God and my husband, my husband was not drawn to my beauty.

Honoring God in all my ways did not come without challenges. I remember going off on my husband one day. I scared him and scared myself. I was upset with him because of an incident that occurred over the phone and because he told me he would spend time with me, but he did not. He was feeling sick, and I wanted to pour the hot Theraflu that he was drinking all over his body. I wanted to sit there and curse him out and hurt him back. I told him he needed to listen to me and that he was upsetting me terribly. He said he would not listen to me and that I was just like my mother. He cursed at me and kept telling me to leave him alone. He even asked kindly, but I refused. What an opportunity this was for me to retaliate. My goodness! What in the world brought me to this point? My heart was becoming hardened. Was I trusting God or not? It seemed like trouble was on every side and *"I have discovered this principle of life – that when I want to do what is right, I inevitably do what is wrong"* (Romans 7:21 NLT). Later that day, that guilt and shame was eating me alive.

Shortly afterwards, as he began to get better, my husband blew off five hundred dollars. This was not the first time an incident like this had occurred. Not only that, but nearly four hundred dollars was charged to the bank credit card. I was upset. We had just caught up from the last time. I was ready to go and save money for a laptop, renew our membership at the grocery store, and order some Christian videos. I also wanted to pay ahead on some phone bills. To say I was furious with his response would be an understatement. When I mentioned all these things to my husband, he acted as though he did not remember what was going on. What happened to the money? After calling our bank, the discovery was made. My husband's credit card that was attached to our joint account had at least $5,100 worth of transactions. He did not admit it until I sat down and told him that I did not believe him and he needed to tell me the truth. I sat and listened as he explained where and how he threw the money away. Maybe despising him was not a good thing. But my emotions were running rampant; I was ready to burst. It seemed as though my labor was in vain. My fight was tiring, and I wanted to cry, curse, scream, and fight all at the same time. Every dime we needed to save was being fed to the wolves. It seemed as though we were working to become poor. Working to help others become prosperous. Working, but not seeing any victorious results.

Although it seemed as if I was playing God's role, lecturing my husband seemed appropriate. Telling him that he had all the resources necessary to get the help he needed but was refusing to utilize them seemed like a way for me to push him to move forward. I did not want to have an explosive situation take place. My thoughts were that if he were to get support from people, mainly the men from the church who were reaching out to him, that maybe our life would be a little better. I questioned the genuineness of my husband's heart when he wanted to do something at church as far as volunteering, because of his pattern of backing out when the time came around. I once again listened to an excuse as to why he could not do it. My goodness, if I was upset from trying to get his attention over the past few years, what was God thinking? I let him know that we needed to pray and read the Bible together. People in the church often say things like "People that pray together stay together." This is something I questioned. At least I could put my trust in Matthew 18:20 (KJV): *"For where two or three are gathered together in my name, there am I in the midst of them."* We needed to attend church together on Sundays, Wednesdays, and maybe on Fridays. He would not listen to me, so I figured that he was slowly beginning to lose sight of God. Not only was he losing sight of God, but he had lost sight and direction of who he was and of his family.

Early one morning, I arrived at home around 6:50 AM, just as my husband was turning off the alarm clock. I went and lay next to him and put my head on his pillow with him, and he turned over on his side away from me. This time, he kept covering his face with the blankets. He would not look at me or speak to me. Yes, I believe I smelled alcohol on his breath. Not that this was unusual, but deep down inside, I hoped that I was the one who was wrong (as far as what I was smelling). The fact that he was behaving in that manner made me suspicious anyway. I told him that he always turned away from me when I wanted to cuddle with him. Not that I expected him to do this, but he then went to the restroom to brush his teeth. When he came back into the room, he was approaching me as if he wanted to try to make it up to me. I told him that when he acted that way, I thought his behavior was very suspicious. I was hoping to provoke an honest response. Although I knew the truth for myself, I just wanted him to be completely honest and admit what he was doing. Moreover, I told myself that although I really knew what the truth was, provoking him was a way of making me feel good, at least for the moment. Knowing the truth and hearing it from him, the offender, was soothing. I felt that there would be no rest for him if I did not get the truth. There would be no peace at all. I could stay up all night if necessary. He was going to feel the pain that I had been feeling.

My husband thought I was always being negative, and I was bringing him down. He said I always dogged him out (meaning I was always fussing about something). I was not giving him room to grow. He did not owe me anything, not even any explanations. He wanted to walk out on me because I did not listen to him, so therefore, he'd had to go outside of the marriage in the past to get support. What exactly did he mean? What kind of woman did he think I was? Now those were fighting words. My heart dropped. Although my mind was racing, I had to keep it together. I could not bite him, burn him, kick him, cut him, strangle him, or anything like that. Support, huh? Oh, I was not the woman, the wife who was going to be a stepping stool, a pushover. He said he was not a liar just because he lies when he is under the influence of alcohol, and that he was not a bad person. Wow! I guess support meant anyone who could please him without asking him questions or holding him accountable for his actions. Anyone who would feed into and approve what he was saying and doing without any consequences – that was the relationship he longed for. That was not me?

Whenever I told him how I felt about something, he would keep saying it was not all about me. But he could tell me how he felt and what he wanted. He yelled and said he did not want to hear my @&*#%! mouth, and that he did not care about anything I said. He told me he could walk out that door anytime he felt like it and I would not have to worry about seeing him again. He told me that I had the same right. He then said that he was leaving for work. Five minutes later, he came back to the room to argue with me. I kinda wished that I had not said anything at all.

Eventually, I had to open a separate account to put money away. He got upset. It broke my heart to have to do that. We were supposed to be a team. We were supposed to be joined together. I wanted to share everything with my husband. I knew that I was doing what was right, but the decision was still painful. I just wish I did not have to dig for answers to my questions regarding our money. I could not say that I trusted him like I had in the past. I just did not know what the truth was anymore. He did not want to tell me the whole truth, just bits and pieces. My husband had now spent at least three thousand dollars on his addiction. This was craziness.

At that point, we were expecting money back from the IRS. This should have gotten us out of a lot of debt from our previous endeavors. From the time I mentioned this information to him, I noticed that he had already withdrawn money from the account. This was done often. I had opened a single savings account and had it attached to a checking account that I had also opened. If only I could see what was in the savings. I did not want to live paycheck to paycheck anymore. He was upset when he first discovered that my direct deposit was no longer going into the joint account. He was just upset that I had not told him all this time. I never felt that I had to explain that.

We were becoming so distant. It was beyond my comprehension, almost, as to why he just did not seem to care about our finances or the uplifting cards I had been giving him. He was not hugging me anymore. He was barely kissing me before going to work. He was not spending time with me or communicating with me. I became a cold-hearted wife. I did not care whether he did those things or not. I just did not care anymore. I did not even care about the dishes not being done, the kitchen not being kept clean, the laundry getting left behind, the lights and television being left on all the time, the restroom not being kept up with, or even the kids always leaving items on the living room floor. I was on a strike for real. If I was not going to get help around the house, then the work was not going to be done. Why waste my breath? Why waste my time?

As time passed by, the anger between my husband and me had spilled over to the children. I was so angry with my husband. So many ideas had crossed my mind, but I could not possibly say or do anything to him when he was down and out and not feeling well (again), although I reminisced about the previous situation. The kids were beginning to express their anger. They began to fight with each other more and talk back to us more. My daughter kept saying that our son was whispering mean things to her. She had placed alphabet stickers on her door that said, "I hate you!" I told her that God did not like that and she needed to take it down.

We began trying to pray together as a family. At one point, I was letting the kids pick out their own scriptures before bedtime. After all the drama, feeling sick, worn down, angry, and overwhelmed, I slowly came back to my senses. God wanted me to enjoy where I was until I got to where He wanted me to be, especially concerning my job. God had to ask me why I was not trusting Him in all things. He said that I knew what He had promised me and my family. I knew what He had promised for our future. If I believed that He was who He said He was, then why was I not trusting and believing that He would do what He said He would do? I was reminded about Jesus and His disciples. When the storm came and they were on the boat, they became troubled amid the storm. They lost sight of who God was (Matthew 8:23-25). God reminded me of how I was looking at the situation and not keeping my eyes on Him.

I remember when one of the elders from the church said, "If you know that Jesus is on your side, then you will know that Jesus will bring you through." There had been so much drama. I was so tired of the physical altercations between my husband and me. I started some of the altercations, and he did too. We both knew better. I knew for myself that God had told me before to praise Him, sing songs, read, or pray in the midst of my circumstances. At times, I chose not to listen to Him. The funny thing is, I knew what to do to beat the enemy.

After a week of fasting, listening to the audio Bible series on the book of Job. I was so tired of the chaos in our house. As I listened and read along in the Bible, God revealed something to me. He showed me Job 3:11-26, which talked about some of Job's troubles and how awful it felt to experience them. Like Job, many of us, including myself, love God and are living righteously, but that does not mean that God will allow Satan to take our lives. God may test us by allowing Satan to come to us and stir things up. Even though times get rough and we want to give up and tell God how miserable we are. God does not want us to look at our situations. God told me that just like Job, all we must do is to keep trusting in Him just as He promised, our latter days will be good. We will see, just as He promised Job, that our latter days will be greater than our past (Job 42:12).

I remember one of the sermons from a church that I attended when I was in Kentucky. It was about creating an atmosphere of praise, prayer, promise, and power. One of the points that was mentioned was "If victory is promised, why give up?" If we endure, will see the prize, the promises in the end. A woman carries a baby for nine months and feels the discomfort of it. As she endures the discomforts and pains, she eventually sees the prize, the promises: her beautiful child or children.

I believed that God wanted the church to know that it is time to kick Satan out of our home. He is to pack his things and go. We cannot allow him to leave anything behind. Do you know why? It is because if he does, he will have a reason to come back and gather up those things he left behind and linger in our homes. Tell the devil to get out and stay out. I was tired of seeing Satan destroy our homes. He *"comes only to steal and kill and destroy"* (John 10:10 NIV). It is time to get serious and stop playing with the devil. We, as a people, better get in our own prayer closets and pray and spend time in the Word and worship. We must get away from all the distractions to hear God speak.

It seemed like God was allowing my husband and me to go through our trials to get us all cleaned up and ready for what He had in store for us. There was a purging going on, and the devil didn't like it. Through our trials, God was taking me back to relive some past experiences. Perhaps it is because people need to be set free by the words of my testimony. God also reminded me that I had been judging others, and unless I wanted to be judged by the same measures I judged others by, I needed to shut my mouth. Because my husband and I were beginning to forget that we were not problem free, God had to take us back through some trials to remind us to keep our mouths off others. Just when we thought we were set free, God showed us new issues that were lying dormant within us. If God takes us to a new level, He wants us to be more mature and put aside ungodly thoughts and actions.

CHAPTER 2
NEW JOB

My husband eventually received a full-time permanent position. For some reason, it was so easy at times to trust in his words. Although I knew what to do and how to do it, he was almost like my personal God. Regardless of what I heard or saw, most of the time, I allowed his persuasive words to convince me. I decided to take his advice and apply for a government job. After applying for several jobs in my county and a few others, I finally received a letter about an interview. During all this chaos, I had a job offer to work for a state facility. This was the beginning of more hardships. But rest assured that there was light at the end of the tunnel. My troubles will not last always. God's promises are unfailing, and as Psalm 119:28 (KJV) says, *"My soul melteth for heaviness: strengthen thou me according to thy word."*

Part of the interview included a physical test. Not too long afterwards, I received a letter asking me whether I would accept the position, giving me the time and date to show up for the orientation, and listing the items I would need to bring for orientation. I was so excited that I was going to have better health insurance, a retirement plan, better pay, and paid vacation and personal time. I had to drive forty-five minutes to my job, but it was worth it. After all, I just knew that I was not going to be there long anyway. My goal was to work through my probation, apply for another job in the county that I lived in, and then work in that county. I was going to do what I had to do and then move on to an even better job.

But my goals were quickly interrupted. Not too long after I finished my orientation, the governor declared a hiring freeze. What is that? This meant that the government agencies were not allowed to hire anyone new due to the state's financial situation. I was stuck! Everyone who was hired around the same time as me had to go through weeks of training. We were then released to work with individuals in the assigned facilities. We had a lead worker and co-workers to guide us. I remember reporting abuse of a resident when I was placed on the unit during the orientation. I was finally placed on the floor (working on the residential units) for good, and I could feel the wrath of those who hated what I had done. How could people sit back and watch and agree with the mishandling of another individual? There was so much more retaliation for what I had done. I was assigned to the medical unit. Taking care of people was always a pleasure to me, but the atmosphere created by the staff was a nightmare. Although I was trained on all three shifts, I ended up being assigned to the night shift. I worked from 10:30 at night until 6:30 in the morning. My co-workers appeared to be stressed out, controlling, angry, bitter, hating their lives, and upset with management – and upset with me just for being at work.

There was an individual who had a room to himself. Although most residents in that area did not exhibit aggressive behavior, the guy I was assigned to did. He knew when new staff sat with him. It was as though he could identify the staff by their scent. One lead worker told me that if I needed any assistance, I could just yell for help. During the early morning hours, this individual became restless and began to chew on his hand mitts until they came off. It was important that I redirect him properly, or I would have taken a chance of injuring myself or him.

After what seemed like hours of constant redirecting, I stepped outside of the room and yelled for help. What a work out this was for me. What in the world had I really signed up for myself in this position? No one came to assist me. When urine and feces were spread in the areas outside of his room and he became boisterous, that was when my help arrived. She said, "I told you if you needed help to just yell!" I stood silently. Is this what my nights were going to look like? Was this first assignment just to break me in, or was it just an act of retaliation for reporting staff when I was in training? One co-worker asked me if I was a secret agent.

Surely, the behavior of the staff towards me lasted long. The supervisors ended up assigning me so much overtime that I wanted to sleep as much as possible during my time off. Those days depended on the rotation schedule. The facility was never fully staffed, and the workers were already overworked. I was told that the best way to keep from being mandated was to sign up for overtime. I just did not understand that method, and I did not trust the words out of the mouths of anyone there.

Light in Darkness

Going to work and managing my personal life was becoming unbearable. It was important for me to learn how to manage both. Sometimes I would be ready to get off work at 6:30 AM, only to find out at 6:00 AM that I had been mandated. This occurred a lot. There were many instances where I wanted to find a hiding place and cry. I had to learn the ropes quickly. No one offered to assist me with getting the residents dressed and ready for breakfast in the dining hall. It was almost unbearable. The nights were long and rough, but although I had many restless nights, I had to push myself psychologically, physically, and mentally. I had to make sure I spent time outside of the home with my kids and tried to keep my marriage intact.

One day, the morning staff came in for work. I had a slight grin on my face as I said, "Good morning!" One lady immediately said with awful language, "I don't know what is so &@*$&# good about this morning." It was at that point that I decided to come to work, stay to myself, and only speak when necessary. How long had the staff been working there? Why did they choose to stay? Was the money so good that they stayed and became so bitter? It appears I had been sentenced to more torment than I had experienced before. My heart towards others was not bad, or at least I didn't think so. What were all these tribulations about? I hated the things I had been through, and I wanted no more troubles myself, but to live a quiet peaceful life.

I had many rough days. Why would this cause me to hate being at the workplace that God blessed me to have? This was a dry place. What a battle – work was a war zone. I told my husband one morning, after he asked for the reason why I got up early, that it was because I needed to read the Bible before entering the war zone of work. He told me to have a good time at work. I told him that I would.

Yes indeed! The warfare around me was great. I know that I have been called by God to stand out as a difference maker. The people I worked with appeared to have so much more animosity and were not compassionate towards some of their fellow coworkers, supervisors, and residents around them. It was almost like it was a burden for them to come to work, and they showed up only because they needed the money and health benefits.

It was difficult to work so many nine-to-fifteen-hour shifts. The overtime that I worked was unheard of. There was so much gossip around me. The residents and staff were behaving the same on most units, to the point that it was difficult to perceive who were the residents and who were the staff. It was as though the staff had been stuck in that place for so long that they were accepting the same behavior in themselves. The staff cursed and threw fits all the time. I went home crying many times. I remember telling God that I did not want to do this. I told God that there was no way that He would want me, His child, to be enduring all of this. I was exhausted all the time. Every time I had a day off, I was relieved, but those days were short lived. My body was wearing down. I was fatigued. My goal was to enjoy my days off, but I also knew the drama that I would face at home. I felt that I had to find more peace in the lesser of the two evils (or situations). Either way, my battles were constant. It was impossible to sleep as much as I wanted to on my days off. My spirit was restless. The days I was at home were mainly filled with arguments due to agitation that came from my husband's addictions and my work experiences. My laughter was few and far between. I regretted going back to work. For each day that I had off, I worked a double or at least four extra hours of overtime, and I had other mandated overtime throughout the week. My schedule did not bother my husband one bit. In my mind, I began to wonder if he would rather have me at work than at home. I was not sure.

I could not wait for both of my fifteen-minute breaks. I looked forward to them desperately. I would go to the break room or my car nearly in tears because I wanted to rest. I feared the wrath of the supervisors and my co-workers, so I did not sleep most of the time. I cried out to God many nights: "What is this awful hell around me? Why me? Why do I have to endure this?" For every day that I had to come in to work, I had also made up in my mind, whenever I had a day off, how I would deal with my job. Each time, I would say, "I quit." I did not believe I was strong enough for this battle. But God's Word says in Psalm 18:39, *"For you have circled me with strength for battle; you have subdued under me those who revolted against me."* I was going through a test – a test that I believed I had already fulfilled. It was as though God were keeping me in a prison and playing a crazy joke on me.

I began to bring books to read overnight, including several books that I'd just purchased and some that I'd always had. My goals were to read them and meditate on them to have peace of mind. It was important that I indulged in the spiritual material. I also began to listen to Christian music as much as possible to help make sense of how the enemy was manifesting in the spiritual realm and deal with it.

At some point, I convinced myself that if I continued to work there, all the darkness that was around me would put my light out. I felt trapped. Someone from my church told me that maybe I was there to be a light. I was there to shine in that place. I may be the only light that the people around me saw. My immediate thought was that there was no way that this was possible. But that put a twist on how I saw things. My eyes of negativity and my heart felt and saw the situation a little bit differently. John 1:5 (NIV): *"The light shines in the darkness, and the darkness has not overcome it."*

God had not forsaken me and would not allow me to go through anything that He believed I would not get through. I had to learn to trust God. I had to know that God would never stop protecting me. This battle was not easy, but what battle is? The fire was turning up. It was up to me to learn how to stay strong in the midst of the fires.

My attitude still needed to be adjusted as I was growing. When Christmas came around, a lady was selling items from her catalog. I decided to participate and to soften my heart a little towards my enemies. I ordered a yellow chicken figurine holding a sign that said, "Do I look like a freaking people person?" I ordered another item that said something like "This isn't PMS, it's my regular attitude." I found humor in those things. They might have appeared to be crude (blunt or offensive) to others, but it was humorous to me.

As time went on, I began to interact with others a little bit more than what was required of me. My trust was not in anyone that I was working with, period. My eyes were open, and I needed to see exactly what was going on with everyone around me. I needed to know what to pray about. My prayer life was being challenged, and I could either pray or complain. Wavering in my faith was easy. I knew that I had to press into God, but following through put a strain on me.

Later rather than sooner, there was a shifting taking place within my spirit, and within my mind. I knew when to speak up and when not to. One day, I was in the dining room feeding a resident. The staff and residents were around as well. As I fed the gentleman, the lead worker on the unit told me that I needed to feed him faster. He wanted me to rush a resident to eat and drink and get him out of the dining hall. He wanted to stick to a quick-fix schedule. I continued feeding the resident at the same pace. My heart was weakening. I wanted to cry. I did not want the staff to see my fear or anger. It was not necessary to continue a conversation about this matter. The residents were not part of a military regiment. Why would any of them be treated as though they needed to eat swiftly? How would I have wanted to be treated if I were in their situation? Why was the staff so heartless? Where was their compassion?

The most unique residents were drawn to my heart. Many times, one bed-ridden resident would pull his feeding tube from his body and have diarrhea. As I would enter the room, he'd be smiling and moaning tirelessly as he tampered with the tube. I thought the world of him, but many did not. Every time he disconnected the tube, the alarm sounded for more than just a moment, and the nurse would have to come into the room. One night, I was in the room with the nurse. She was attending to him, and she looked at me and said, "Boy, I will be glad when he dies." I stared at her in shock and then I told her that I really liked him. I enjoyed taking care of him and seeing him smile.

With work and family issues happening, I looked forward to some time off, for what that was worth. I was tired of crying and fighting. My shoulders were heavy. Matthew 11:28-30 (ESV) says, *"Come to me, all who labor and are heavy laden, and I will give you rest. Take my yoke upon you, and learn from me, for I am gentle and lowly in heart, and you will find rest for your souls. For my yoke is easy, and my burden is light."* It was close to the time for another Joyce Meyer conference, and I could not wait. The first one was so powerful and enlightening. I felt as though I could conquer the world afterwards. My strength was renewed. My house was never going to be the same. My marriage was going to be different. My outlook on situations was not going to be the same. I felt the fire of God. It was as though I was super empowered and could, as Brain would say on the cartoon *Pinky and the Brain*, "try to take over the world."

I got together with a small group of women from church, and we drove to a hotel that was near the bridge to downtown Missouri. I was expecting a mighty move of God again. Worship and singing praises unto God were things I enjoyed. After the first day of the conference, I drove back to the hotel with the ladies. I remember the lady I shared rooms with walking up, and she was itching or had felt a bite. Well, it turned out to be a bed bug bite. What in the world? This was not something I was familiar with. I googled how bedbugs operated. How did they get into the room? This was not scary for me. After all, I grew up with roaches, lizards, snakes, cats, dogs, frogs, worms, and much more. When I was younger, my mother used to say "Goodnight! Don't let the bed bugs bite." And when the lady mentioned bed bugs, I began to reminisce about the days of old. Who came up with the saying? What was the meaning and what was the purpose? The lady I shared the room with did not crack one smile. She was quite upset. After making a complaint at the front desk, we were able to get another room.

As I lay down to sleep, I only thought of what was going on at home. The lady I was sharing the room with had called her husband earlier and prayed together over the phone as she kneeled by her bed. I began to have an overwhelming feeling of guilt because I did not do what they were doing. My hope was that my husband and I would be more connected to Christ. Although the Word of God says to *"Take therefore no thought for the morrow: for the morrow shall take thought for the things of itself. Sufficient unto the day is the evil thereof"* (Matthew 6:34 KJV), I fell asleep worrying about my husband and my children. While I was at home, I was the protector and the person who helped keep the order.

The next day, we headed back to the conference. I was hoping someone would volunteer to drive. We used my car to travel, but only one lady said she would be willing to drive, and she was not such a good driver in the Missouri area. I remember thinking to myself, "Why am I using my car, driving around with these ladies, and reserving the rooms for my friends or so-called friends, who are using me as a taxi driver? Why would they take advantage of me, and why am I allowing this? What were Christians, rooted and grounded in Christ Jesus, supposed to be like?"

This conference was the second of two that I had attended. In the first session, Creflo Dollar spoke on how to stay in the faith. He spoke on many things. One interesting thing he said was that when you need a breakthrough, you need a word from God. You will have to overcome old mindsets to be promoted. Old mindsets, huh? I was not so sure that was an easy thing to do.

In another session, Joyce Meyer spoke. Her topic was "The Power of One." One of the things I learned was that you cannot give away what you do not have – one of her examples was love. And if revival was going to start, it would have to start in my home, with me. And if I believed in what I have, I would need to start developing it. When I left the conference, I had a lot to think about.

Somehow, I got wind of the Axis Conference in Fenton, Missouri. This was a prophetic conference. My hunger for the things of God was high, so I attended the conference. The worship team and prophetic team were on fire. As they called out for prayer and prophetic words to be given, I thought I would get in line. I had been introduced to prophecy before, and I needed a rhema word, a specific word from the Lord. One of the things that was spoken over me was "Be careful who you follow, I've made you a leader." He also said, from the Lord, that it was a miracle for me to be there "tonight." Greater levels, greater devils! Many times, church folks would say this as they spoke to someone to warn of the fight ahead as they grew in Christ and sought out God. Even though I had a basic understanding of the phrase, I did not understand the magnitude of the "power" of the force of the devils.

As I continued to work, go to church, and attend conferences, it seemed as though every devil in hell were out to revolt against me. The warfare outweighed the fight. I was reading the Word, praying, and worshipping God, and getting worn out all at the same time. I began to work more overtime than I cared to have worked. The workers were getting injured more on the job.

Residents had unexplained injuries. Supervisors brought their personal issues to work with them. My household was still out of whack. Everything I believed God for was challenged. I questioned God many times. Was I a good mother? Was I a good wife? Was I a good enough Christian? God, why are you doing this?

CHAPTER 3
CAR ACCIDENT

Just when I thought I was breaking through and expecting that God was going to get me out of my impossible situations, I was assigned more mandatory overtime. I was so overwhelmed, and I barely saw my kids at all. I would get home some days just to get them off to school. I wanted to visit them at their schools, but sometimes I was too tired to do that. One weekend, having a few days off, I decided to take the kids to yard sales with me. They were excited to go look at fun stuff to buy. They got into my new van and sat together in the third row, in the very back. I had purchased the van so they could sit separately and no one would have to worry about who was on their side of the seat or who was touching who. But for some reason, that day, they decided to sit together.

I stopped by the ATM before making our first stop. I did not have anything special in mind as to what to purchase, but the kids and I were going shopping around. There was a neighborhood near their school that had some sales going on. As I was waiting to turn into the neighborhood, I was on the phone with a woman from church. Before I had the opportunity to make a turn, I felt a huge jolt. My phone was no longer in my hand. I yelled. I was in shock as I sat shaking and wondering where my phone was. One of the kids handed it to me. The impact of a vehicle that crashed into me had caused my phone to end up in the rear seat with the kids. The children screamed a little. As my fingers gripped the steering wheel firmly, I looked to my left and right, and a gentleman came up to the car and asked if everyone was OK. He recommended that I move the van to prevent it from getting hit again. When the paramedics arrived, one of them stuck their hand through the driver side window and turned the car off.

Well, this added to my frustrations. I knew my husband was home wasted, and the individual I was on the phone with ended up calling him. When my husband arrived at the hospital, I awakened to see him standing over me. I was fairly upset with him. I could smell the alcohol on his breath. Our daughter was in one room and I was in the other. My son said he was simply fine, but that was probably because he had seen his friend walking down the sidewalk with his mother at the time of the accident. I knew that the money I had taken out to spend was already in the hands of my husband. I already knew, but there were going to be a ton of excuses as to where the money went to. One peaceful day was all I was looking for. This was my weekend off. How many more heartaches were to come?

Time Off

Great! I needed and pleaded for time off from work, but, my God, this happened in the strangest way. When I was released to go back home, I called my supervisor to let her know that I was involved in a car accident and would not be in. Although I was hesitant to make that phone call because of the fear of being retaliated against, it was necessary. I feared that they were going to try to tell me that I needed some type of proof that I had to be off, and that I needed to give them more of an advance notice and would have to come to work as soon as possible. There was total silence on the other end before the on-duty supervisor finally responded. It was at that time that I believed that they felt a little bit of condemnation and possibly believed that they were at fault for pushing the overtime on me.

My husband, kids, and I went home. I needed to rest, period. Rest did not come easy at home, but I sure was hoping that maybe my husband would see this as a moment when he could have lost his family. Despite the accident, though, my time off really was not time off. This was now a time when I had to face my home life and go to multiple appointments on the road to recovery. This was scary for me. Would my husband care for me the way I would care for him? I was in a sticky situation. Maybe I would earn the compassion, but I needed it for speedy, speedy, speedy recovery. Looking on the bright side of things, at least I could see the children more and spend more alone time with God. This was a vital part of my healing.

As days passed by, I dealt with various aches and pains and appointments. My routines involved getting up with the kids, doctor visits, watching cooking shows, feeding my spiritual man, and sleeping. After a while, I was beginning to feel lonely. My husband worked full time. Everyone (for the most part) worked during the day, so there were not too many people I could call on or visits I could make. I felt so alone. It seemed like I did not have a friend indeed. It was as though I was in a world all by myself. Where in the world were my friends? Why wasn't anyone calling to check on me?

My schedule was the same nearly each day and week. I only went grocery shopping every thirty days. I did not like shopping during the winter at all, so I made sure there was enough food in the deep freezer in the basement, on the shelves, and in the refrigerator. I only grabbed food and drinks and condiments from the stores when necessary. As time passed, I began to prepare dinner after watching the food shows. I would print interesting recipes. My intentions were to try to stay busy, please my husband, and have new food ideas for the kids. There were products that I hadn't heard of that the cooks or shows spoke about. I took pride in cooking, but afterwards, the pain in my body seemed so unbearable.

Physical therapy was not fun, and I hated taking pills. The pain was so bad that nothing could stop it from going away. Now I had more misery and tears to add to my life. Besides my appointments, I was pretty much trapped in my own house. It appears I was being tormented by God, the devil, or both to be taught a lesson. My husband was doing well at work, and I felt jealous of him. He was able to get out, talk to friends, go to work, and do whatever he wanted to do while I suffered. I longed for him to be at home. I was in a dreamy world, hoping that this one incident was going to change our lives forever, in a good way. But as soon as he came home, hell and its fury often came along with him. The house was turned upside down in many ways. Although he appreciated the new meals I cooked to show my appreciation for him, his politeness and appreciation towards me were short lived. Curse words and reckless speech flowed from his mouth. I hated being ripped apart. At the same time, there was nothing that my heart and mind were not used to. It was almost acceptable if I kept quiet or walked away peacefully.

I did my best to do some cleaning around the house, but my body screamed in agony during or after sitting up, standing, and lying down. It was painful. Living was dreadful to me. I was watching Pastor Benny Hinn and Apostle Guillermo Maldonado during the daytime, and sometimes I would watch Joyce Meyer too. I was drawn to Apostle Maldonado and Pastor Hinn because they operated in the supernatural. I figured that if they were genuine, and if those people were really getting healed, then perhaps God could do that for me. I began to google their itineraries to see if they would be coming to an area near me, and if so, where. I wanted to go even if that meant getting on an airplane. I had never been on a plane before and never had any interest in flying, but I was desperate, and I wanted healing. Luke 8:43-48 describes a woman with the issue of blood. She had suffered for twelve long years, and she was desperate like I was. She decided to press through a crowd of people to touch the hem of Jesus' garment. She was made whole.

Day after day, I watched and listened to the two men. My desire for healing and freedom increased. My attitude changed from hoping for the things that I was seeing to trusting God and believing God for total healing. I was excited.

As I watched TV throughout the day, I was seeing commercials regarding the Holy Land tours to Israel. Israel was one of the two places that I had always wanted to visit, along with Haiti. On the first spiritual television channel I had been watching, I saw a commercial about getting free information, which included a DVD about Israel, the different landmarks, and the sites to see. I decided to call the phone number that was on the television screen. Even though I could not see how God was going to make a way financially or how He would provide for my family while I attended, I was just longing to be in the place where Jesus breathed, walked, lived, healed, died, and much more. The tour would include ten days of experience. If God is God, if God was healing those people on TV and setting them free, then surely God was going to give me the desires of my heart.

Boy, I wished I were amid their presence. The anointing was in their environment. The Lord was meeting the needs of His people. Those people came just as they were. Hungry! Desperate! Hopeless! They came expecting God to move on their behalf. I remember wanting to cry because I could see the miracles, signs, and wonders taking place. I was anxious, and I thought to myself, "When will I have a turn?" I would have jumped through the TV if I knew I could just enter their environment where the Holy Spirit was dwelling so richly. I wanted the experience those people had. According to Psalm 34:8 (TLB), *"Oh, put God to the test and see how kind he is! See for yourself the way his mercies shower down on all who trust in him."* God sure was being good to them. I could just taste and see.

God, Where Are You?

God, where are you? I cannot see you! I cannot feel you! I cannot hear you! I do not know which direction to go! Who can I trust? Surely, I did desire the freedom and healing that I had seen on TV. And, as far as my marriage, my husband and I sought advising and counseling from trusted couples and individuals from our local church at that time. We started with one couple or individual, and then we moved on to the next, then the next, then... So, we had gone through nearly every leader, friend, and frenemy that we knew.

People said they would pray for us, but were they? What did their prayers consist of? Who was really for us? It seemed that the more we put our hope and trust in people, the more things got out of hand. Not everyone who was around us was for us. I was troubled by the amount of unreliable, untrustworthy folks who were in our circle. Some people were only sticking by my husband's side and mine to gather information and gossip. There were wolves in sheep's clothing on a mission to destroy my marriage. I wondered how many people we had confided in actually spoke negatively about us but didn't know that the words they were releasing were actually curses from their mouths. The encouragement that was released to us, to our faces, was voided out by the gossip about us. Proverbs 16:28 (ISV) says, *"A deceitful man stirs dissension, and anyone who gossips separates friends."*

We had gotten to the point where we were tired of listening and talking to all these people. There were too many opinions and different advice from everyone. I felt that my husband and I needed to set time aside from everything just to be alone with God and listen to Him. There was so much noise in our ears that we could hardly decipher God's voice.

On the other hand, I could only see parts of God's plans coming together, but my feelings were still in the way. And how could I get past all the hurts, the pain, and the bitterness towards my husband? What about all those women, whoever they were, that I may or may not have even known, who were in and out of his life? I wanted to know what it would take for him to see me as his best friend, not his enemy. There was always a reminder or two (or more) of the things that would aggravate my hurt. It appears my emotions and my spirit were scarred. How was I supposed to pray for my husband or for anyone else? What kind of encouragement was I supposed to speak over anyone else, especially a woman? How many of them were in my life, but mocking me at the same time? Which of them were double agents, pretending to be my friend, but actually closer to my husband? How was I supposed to truly, genuinely care about my husband and about being a couple? How was I supposed to do all these things as a wife? When you feel that you have given your all, there is nothing else to give.

God was not only dealing with my husband and his ways, but He was certainly dealing with me and my ways as well. I kept losing sight of God. I was not sanctifying my husband. Because of that, the children were not being sanctified. As the believing, stronger vessel, I had a job to do, and I was lacking (1 Corinthians 7:14 KJV).

I kept hearing song lyrics like "God is able to do what He said He would do" and "It isn't over until God says it's over." But sometimes I just got tired. It was as though I was going around and around in circles as part of a vicious game. I just wanted to be happy and for my kids to be happy and for all of us to be healed. I know that that we (my family) were hoarding so much anger and bitterness inside. How could I have changed to help them during those storms? I hurt with and for them.

I could no longer trust advice from those around us. Some people could not comprehend what we were dealing with because they had not lived such challenges. They were offering suggestions and opinions based merely on their own ideas; although there were some people who were genuine, they were making suggestions that were not what God wanted for me and my husband.

CHAPTER 4
DIVORCE! DIVORCE! DIVORCE!

Wₑ had opened the doors and invited many people into our marriage. Now I had gotten to the point where my mind was made up again: "I'm moving!" What was this roller coaster all about? One minute I was happy; the next minute I was doubtful. Then I was hopeful, and then I was excited. What was causing me to be unstable and movable? I remember crying out to God. I recalled the voices of a few ladies. One asked me why I was not leaving my husband. She said she did not see how I had not ended up in a nuthouse. The other lady said, at a different point in time, that there was no way she could put up with it. I just thought that some people were not built to weather the storm. I was in a fight for my marriage and for my family. But talk is cheap!

At some point, though, I thought that enough was enough. This storm was too much. I'd borne all things. I could not do this marriage anymore. I went down to the courthouse and got a divorce packet. I filled out all the paperwork and hid it in my clothes drawer. I just figured it was time for me to pack my things and go. My husband was not happy, and I was not happy. I did not care to be happy with him anymore.

I was tired of being the stronger one. I wanted to gather all his clothes and throw them in the backyard. I was ready to have a bonfire – just me, myself, and I. No one else was invited. The Bible says in 1 Corinthians 10:13 (AMP), *"No temptation [regardless of its source] has overtaken or enticed you that is not common to human experience [nor is any temptation unusual or beyond human resistance]; but God is faithful [to His word – He is compassionate and trustworthy], and He will not let you be tempted beyond your ability [to resist], but along with the temptation He [has in the past and is now and] will [always] provide the way out as well, so that you will be able to endure it [without yielding, and will overcome temptation with joy]."*

I remember going downstairs to the basement one evening. My eyes were filled with tears. I cried out to God and asked Him to please hold on to me and not let me lose my mind. My life was a wreck. There were too many signs of affairs. The addiction was overtaking my husband, and the effects were spreading like a disease. I had spent too much time driving around town looking for my husband and perhaps a woman he may have been with. Maybe he was drunk at a bar. Maybe someone beat him up and left him for dead. I loved and cared for him, but there was so much agony. Why would he do this to us? Why not just leave us alone so he could do as he wished and continue to fulfill the desires of his heart? Was everything that I was thinking or feeling or seeing just a figment of my imagination?

God spoke to me. He told me that I had to pray for him. As I quieted down before the Lord, he showed me that my husband was dying at a strange house. He told me to PRAY! I was shaken by the voice of the Lord. This was a matter of life or death. If I did not pray and cover my husband, he was going to die. I had a choice. I had to lay my bitterness aside and obey the Lord, or be stubborn and disobedient and let him die. For a split second, I thought that maybe he would be better off if I did not intercede for his life. Maybe he and I and the children would all be put out of our misery.

That evening, a special guest from another city was scheduled to speak at our church. I had to work on putting my face back together. My eyes and face needed a makeover. I had to put on a smiling face and pretend that I was doing simply fine. Before going to church, I had to take out my spiritual mask and put it on to cover up my pain.

The event was nearly halfway over when I arrived. Jason was the name of the speaker, and he was an established guy, a radio host. After he was introduced, I had these thoughts in my mind that he was going to be so boring. Surely, he was going to put me to sleep. He was probably there just to show off. After listening to him for at least ten minutes, though, my eyes were enlightened. This guy was interesting. He had something good to say – he was bringing something to the table. I could not believe what Jason was saying. I was no longer tired; he had my full attention. I could not believe what he was saying. Jason had an awesome testimony. He spoke about how God had saved his marriage. I never would have thought he had had any issues – in my eyes, he was super-anointed and a powerful man of God – but he had many challenges in his past. He was humbled enough to speak life and hope by the power of his words, his testimony of what Jesus had done in his life.

Revelation 12:11 (KJV) describes that *"they overcame him by the blood of the Lamb and by the word of their testimony."* It appears that Nancy D. Collins, the author of *Talkin' Out* the House, agreed with this scripture when she stated in chapter 7 of her book, under "Family Ties" in the section titled "Childish Things," that "We do cause others to overcome by the words of our personal testimonies. Praise God!" At the end of the event, I went home to soak in the awesomeness. Sometimes we see people how they are without knowing the cost they had to pay to get where they are. Once again, if God did it for Jason and his wife, truly God was going to do it for me. God is not a God of just one or two chances, but a graceful God of many chances.

God had shown me visions of a new husband. I really could not understand the true interpretation, though. Was it a new physical husband or a new spiritual husband? I did want my husband to be restored. I was trying to remain hopeful.

One evening, my husband, kids, and I were headed to a Friday evening church service that we had been attending as often as possible. My daughter and I had gone ahead of my husband and son. I parked the car on the side of the building, and my daughter and I got out of the car. As she went indoors and I walked around the front, an older gentleman and a woman who was probably in her mid-forties were out front talking. The gentleman, whose name was Thomas, was a bit intoxicated. As I looked at both, they smiled at me and said hi. Thomas made an "oooooweee" sound as he looked at me. He said, "Girrrl! What is your name?" I smiled it off. Then I told him my name, and he then said, "Girl, are you married?" I told him, "Yes, I am." He then asked me if I had a sister. He continued to laugh and goof off and drool a little bit over how attractive he thought I was.

Thomas ended up coming to the ministry almost regularly. I remember showing up sometimes for band/choir rehearsal, and he would see that the church doors were open and invite himself in. Sometimes he would show up with a guitar and interrupt rehearsal. I rendered him harmless. Other Fridays came around, and he would show up still intoxicated. Sometimes he would be nearly emotional and in tears. He had just had a rough day. I remember speaking into his life one day. He seemed so down and depressed. As I stood on the stage for a Friday night pre-service rehearsal, holding a mic in my hand, he came up the stairs, and I told him face to face that he was destined for greatness. I told him that God had awesome plans for his life. He looked at me and his eyes widened as he stood in shock and said, "For real?" I said, "Yes!" He said, "Thank you." He was glad that I saw what God saw in him, because he could not see it for himself.

As he continued to show up during our rehearsals, he shared some things even in his drunken state. He told me that he used to be a preacher, and that he just had some problems. He said that he used to play the guitar as well. Sometimes it is hard to decide whether or not to believe a person based upon what they look or smell like. But I chose to believe everything that he was telling me. He was a great man; he had just fallen by the wayside. I believed that in due time, Thomas was going to be raised, and God was going to restore the things that he had lost. So, if I could strongly believe this for Thomas, maybe I was blinded by my emotions as far as the hope for my husband and for myself. Sometimes it is easier to believe God for someone else. Perhaps that is because of the lack of trauma with the relationship history with others.

If You Can't Beat 'Em, Join 'Em

Somehow, I had learned of a book called *Prayers that Rout Demons* written by Apostle John Eckhardt. I began to fast, pray, and read the book. Had I known then what I know now, I would have prepared myself for the tests that were lying ahead. Just from reading the book, I believe I was speaking to and challenging devils. What level of authority did I have for the principalities? Turmoil was all around me. Church life was rocky. Women were swarming around my husband. I was trying to be strong and not lose my mind.

Although I was praying, worshipping, encouraging others, and being patient with trying to be the glue that kept my family and others together, it just was not working. Every time I read through the book, I was being challenged by the words that I was reading into the atmosphere. It was as though every principality got together to see if I could stand on every word that I had been praying from the book.

Well, there I was again, giving up on God. I was done with church and church folk. This fight was too much. Forget trying to be the strong Christian mother, wife, and saint. I believed I had fought the good fight of faith, and God had suddenly disappeared. I did my best to pour into others, especially those struggling with addiction, in their marriage, and with hopelessness. I am not going to church anymore. Forget it! If folks were not willing to leave the street life, and if the saints were not being genuine, then why did I need to go through all of this? If you can't beat 'em, join 'em!

Some of my closest relatives lived in Kentucky. We visited at least two times a year. One time we visited and let the kids stay. It had been a few weeks since we had dropped our kids off in Kentucky, and I found myself with a strong desire to do research on cocaine, crack, and prostitution. So many people were caught up in this. I began to look up information about different sexual items and performances. I wanted to find out as much as I could; I visited many stores online. After all that research, I began to look at porn, and I began to crave and act out on some of these things. When I read parts of the online book that had the words "8 ball" included in the title, I was drawn in. A strange infatuation came over me. There was so much detail about how to get into prostitution and how crack cocaine worked. I began to feel and become deeply drawn into the experiences that the lady in the article had described. I started reading the information and then went to bed for at least eight hours. I then went back online to continue reading.

Once again, I became deeply drawn into the process. I wanted sexual encounters so bad, with anyone, male, or female. I wanted to try cocaine/crack, and I wanted to walk into the prostitution world. I felt that way for three days, especially when my husband was out of the house. How in the world did I have this sudden interest in getting into the world of prostitution, pimping, homosexuality, and fighting?

Although I was still upset with my husband, I did my best to fulfill his needs. That was one way to fulfill my lusts, and to keep me from looking up George's phone number and address. He was someone I worked with a while back and had begun to daydream about. In my head, I felt that he could fulfill my sexual desires. The desires were so intense that I could not leave the house for fear that I would sleep with the first guy that I would encounter on the streets. If any man (especially) or woman had approached me with a smile or given me a compliment, I would have been ready for a passionate night with them.

After speaking with my husband about this whole ordeal, it seemed he could not handle it. He began to saturate/intoxicate his mind even more with alcohol to deal with it. We began to kill one another with words that were so ungodly. He almost saw me as a perfect person, so my actions and words were unbelievable. My thoughts and behavior were very unusual for him.

I had gone back to the website several times to get more detailed information. Even though my intentions were to get information to help others, I was fooling myself. I had gotten caught up in a crazy spiritual online world. I remember walking through the house searching and having an extraordinarily strong intense feeling and craving for cocaine. I had never used it, but my body was screaming for it. I could almost taste it. I searched the cabinets in the kitchen and began to act nervously as if my body depended on it. What was happening to me?

I remember thinking to myself that I couldn't go to the women's group on Thursdays at the church because I just couldn't leave the house. I would have fallen for the first person who approached me. I couldn't answer the door for the mail carrier or delivery guy because I would've been sure to pull them in, male or female, and do a little bit more than flirting with them. I wanted to have sex with any man or woman, do drugs, perform various sexual acts, get into pornography, drink alcohol, and anything that the street life would offer me.

Something had gotten into me, something that I could not control. I had to stop going to that website and other websites as well. This demon was affecting my mind and my desires so bad. In 1 John 2:16 (KJV), the Word of God says, *"For all that is in the world, the lust of the flesh, and the lust of the eyes, and the pride of life, is not of the Father, but is of the world."* Galatians 5:16 (KJV) says, *"This I say then, Walk in the Spirit, and ye shall not fulfill the lust of the flesh."* It was obvious that I was not walking in the Spirit because I was fulfilling the lust of the flesh.

CHAPTER 5
GOD SPEAKS

As I began to work on the lust of my flesh, I noticed strange things with my vision. Not only was I tired all the time from the medication that I was taking, but something spiritually was going on around me. Many times, I would lie down and take a nap. Upon awakening, I could feel the supernatural presence of something standing over me. In most cases, I would awaken in such fear. I would open my eyes slowly, as a child would in a scary movie. I did not know what was standing there waiting for me. It was as if someone had broken into my house and was hiding in the room. I had to convince myself that everything was OK and that no one was there.

I would begin to play worship music or sing a song. That would keep my mind focused instead of worrying. I would even go down the hallway and walk very cautiously as though I was expecting someone to jump out and spook me. I knew that the activities that were going on in the house were because my husband and I had both allowed the presence of demonic forces to enter our house.

Sometimes, I would go downstairs, but I could not go all the way down without turning the lights on along the way. The washer and dryer were downstairs. Slowly, I would creep down the stairs, turning my head and body because I was wondering who or what was going to be down there waiting for me. Sometimes when I got into my van to drive to my appointments, I would look in the mirror and see silhouettes in the back rows. I had gotten to the point to where I did not want to look in my rearview mirror anymore. I did not want to see anything.

That was the exact same presence that was in my home. When I was there, I could not have any light around me, not at any point. Things were getting worse. On a nice sunny day, I could not open the curtains. I just could not let that light shine through my house. It seemed like my hands were tied when I wanted to open the curtains. It was like the darkness was taking over the house and keeping me trapped within. I wanted that light to shine, but I did not have the mental energy or the will to open those curtains.

I remember crying out to God and asking Him to help me out of this again. What had I gotten myself into? What were those silhouettes that appeared in my car and in my house? Why were they everywhere that I went? Who could possibly help me answer these questions? Who would believe this story? I was operating outside of my norm. But there had to be an end to all the craziness. Enough was enough. I had become ensnared by the traps of the enemy, and so had my husband. We were living in the same house but were living separately. We were total strangers. Life had gotten the best of me, and God was silent.

Encounter

At this point, I began to press into God. Psalm 107:6 (NKJV) reads, *"Then they cried out to the Lord in their trouble, and He delivered them out of their distresses."* I began to cry out once again in desperation. I was beyond feeling hopeless. One day, as I was watching T.D. Jakes on television, I remember feeling as though my hands were tied or bound. I was sure that God had given up on me again, since He seemed to be nowhere around. I had to push myself to clean the house, write, cook on a regular basis, pray, read the Word of God, and get other things done. But then, my world began to shift suddenly. After hours, days, weeks, and months of hell on earth, suddenlies of God arrived, quick and without warning. My (seemingly) unanswered prayers, deliverance, true hope was here. My life was being revived.

One morning, I woke up and walked down the hallway only to see a huge angel in the living room. Even though I paused for a second, I was excited. The feeling that I had was nothing like the times when the dark silhouettes were appearing. A breaking was taking place. It was nice to be able to let the light shine in my house. I could open the curtains again, finally.

As I listened to T.D. Jakes teaching on "Divine Strategies: Creative Tactics for Spiritual Warfare," one of the things that he said was "God is about to untie your hands." I felt like I needed to listen to the message repeatedly. There was so much encouragement from listening to him. I could finally hear and feel God again. He said things like "The enemy comes against you because you are effective. The enemy is trying to wear you out since he cannot hold you down. Satan will use whatever is in your heart to attack you." And finally, he said, "God is going to untie your hands, your visions, and your resources." Well, hallelujah! I said, "Hallelujah!"

A lady I used to associate with at my old church told me of an event at her church called Encounter. She swore up and down it was a time of healing and refreshing. She told me that people would leave changed. I thought that I would grab ahold of it. She was going to attend, and I wanted to go too. I was beyond desperate. However, it cost some money to go; I could not spare that money at the time, and no one could sponsor me. I had to wait until the next enrollment period.

I then felt that God was doing some more work within me, and that He never intended for me to go to the event with that familiar crew that I had been around. But when the next opportunity arose, I was given a chance to attend, so I went. There were several different sessions that allowed for individuals to share their testimonies. While there, I recall telling God that I was determined to be changed and I did not want to "leave here the same, so you're going to have to do something with me while I'm here." I had heard prophetic words released over me. One lady told me that I was so tall like a strong tower. She said that I would help many people and that I was strong. That was an awesome start.

I remember a video that was played. One thing that caught my ears was "Forgiving others is like giving to them what

God gives to you." That is something I had to really ponder. I had to make a list of people I was holding hostage and being unforgiving towards, whether it was my husband, my uncle, myself, my mother, my sisters, or anyone else. This was a time for me to walk in freedom. I had to loose them and let them go. Sometimes we do not know that deep down inside we hold people captive. And while holding them captive, we are also holding ourselves captive.

I learned that I had to speak the Word of God over my life. I learned that it was time for me to close the doors of destruction. God wanted me to be strong. Encounters was freedom away from all the mess that had gone on around me for a long time. It was just a time for women to get together and seek God's face and be healed. I knew that by the time I left, God had healed me in more than one way. Encounters was so awesome.

There were so many women who were drunk in the Spirit and had the gift of tongues. Physical healings were taking place. I saw with my own eyes the lady who arrived in a wheelchair and left pushing it. This was awesome. This was one of the experiences that I'd seen on television when I watched Pastor Benny Hinn. It was happening right before my eyes for the first time.

I realized that I had caused more grief for myself by holding people bondage by walking in unforgiveness. I remember one individual who laid hands on me and spoke a prophetic word over me, telling me that it was time for me to get out of the driver's seat and let God get into it. She told me that I needed to let God be in control. I had been in the driver's seat for so long. Oh my goodness! It was time for me to let God have His way and not be the one who was in control. I remember seeing a cloud hovering over my body as two of the women prayed for me. What an awesome experience this was for me. This was exactly what I needed and exactly what I was looking for.

As we left the facility where Encounter was held, I was so filled with joy, and I was ready to tell the entire world what God had done in my life. I was ready to lay hands on the sick and see them recover. I was ready to raise the dead. The joy of the Lord was my strength. I saw and had hope that I had not had for a long time. My frustrations were not as usual. I no longer wanted to get in the face of others just because they stole my parking spot. I no longer had the lusts of the flesh. Bonfires, no way!

My marriage had to be viewed differently. My mind had to be different regarding my workplace. It was important that I had the mind of Christ in all situations. I could no longer focus on "what-ifs." I could not think about the maybes. I had to totally trust God. I could not lean on my own understanding. No matter what, I had to lean on and trust God. After all, I was now out of the driver's seat. Surely, we would have challenges ahead of us. But Proverbs 3:5-6 (NKJV) says, *"Trust in the Lord with all your heart, and lean not on your own understanding; in all your ways acknowledge Him, and He shall direct your paths."* It was up to me to lean on God and acknowledge Him in all my ways so that He could direct my path.

The hunger and thirst that I had for worshipping my Lord was enormous. I wanted to worship, worship, and worship my God more and more. When I got home, I started my morning by blasting my music and praising God. It did not matter who was asleep, I just wanted to praise the Lord.

People at church even noticed that there was something different about me. After I finished the post-encounter classes, the Lord was using me to prophesy into the lives of others. I could see how God was using other people even when they could not see it for themselves. God had opened my eyes and ears and He was using me, and I was willing to allow Him to.

Man! How did I not know, all these years, that unforgiveness was really what was making me sick? I thank God that those women fasted and prayed on my behalf. I thank God that I did not listen to all the ungodly advice that was given to me. Thank God I did not give up on my marriage. I thank God that He allowed me to experience Him in a totally different way. I learned to go through my house and anoint and pray over every entry point of it. I commanded aches and pains to leave my body whenever they arose. I paid close attention to my dreams. I began to prophesy over my family. God was doing a great work in us, but we had to allow Him to do so.

When God is truly allowed to be in the midst of our situations, there is no room for hopelessness. A hopeless mind is the devil's playground. Let your hope be in Christ Jesus according to Psalm 33:20-22. Marriage is work, and other trials, tribulations, and turbulent storms may come to shake our lives. Through your storms, God is always in control. As you strive to build your relationship with God, He will cause you to be moved, propelled to a different place, a place of healing and maturity. Press into God and trust that He is your everlasting hope. He is not a God that will fail you. You are being propelled to greatness, and He is your hope through turbulent storms.

WORKS CITED

The Bible, KJV, NKJV, NIV, AMP, NLT, ESV, TLB.

Collins, Nancy D. *Talkin' Out the House: A Voice of Hope and Healing.* Ensley House Publishing, 2003.

Dandridge, Marissa. *Uprooted: A New Creation in Christ Jesus.* Heavenly Enterprises Midwest, 2018.

Eckhardt, *John. Prayers That Rout Demons and Break Curses. Lea,* Charisma House, 2010.

Kendrick, Alex, and Stephen Kendrick. *The Love Dare.* Revised edition, B&H Books, 2020.

Meyer, Joyce. *A Leader in the Making: Essentials to Being a Leader After God's Own Heart.* Warner Books, FaithWords, 2002.

"Replant." *Merriam-Webster.com Dictionary*, Merriam-Webster, https://www.merriam-webster.com/dictionary/replant. Accessed 26 Oct. 2020.

"Turbulent." *Merriam-Webster.com Thesaurus*, Merriam-Webster, https://www.merriam-webster.com/thesaurus/turbulent. Accessed 26 Oct. 2020.

www.ingramcontent.com/pod-product-compliance
Lightning Source LLC
Chambersburg PA
CBHW071745090426
42738CB00011B/2575